Now You're Cooking
...with Laughs!

Authentic Creole Recipes from the Old South—by "MOTHER ROUX"

PELICAN PUBLISHING COMPANY

GRETNA 1981

Library of Congress Cataloging in Publication Data

Mother Roux.
    Now you're cooking--with laughs!

    1. Cookery, Creole.   2. Cookery, American--
Louisiana.   I. Title.
TX715.M9182   641.59763   81-17819
ISBN 0-88289-296-7   AACR2

Manufactured in the United States of America

Published by Pelican Publishing Company, Inc.
1101 Monroe Street, Gretna, Louisiana   70053

 Contents

favorite recipes   9-19

seafood   21-34

meat & poultry   35-53

misc. & desserts   55-75

kitchen kuties   77-80

The recipes in this book are genuine and delicious. But "Mother" believes laughs are also a good recipe for people, so she threw in a few . . . which you may throw back out again, if you're a sour-puss!

ORIGIN OF CREOLE COOKING

Creole Cooking is the offspring of French and Spanish parents—with some Indian and African second cousins thrown in for spice and flavor!

It originated in New Orleans where the foods distinctive to Creole cooking grow in abundance—okra, red beans, peppers, rice, herbs and seasonings.

Creole cuisine, in fact, made New Orleans dining famous the world over. So give it a try. It's more fun when you do it yourself!

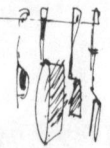

MOTHER'S ROUX

Ninety percent of Creole cooking begins with a French Roux. The other ten percent does not. The dictionary defines Roux as—'a cooked mixture of flour and butter used to thicken soup and sauces'—but there is much more to a good Roux than this feeble description. Roux is a skillful blending and browning of all-purpose flour in hot butter, oil or fat until it is a golden or dark brown. We know of some recipes that even call for a white Roux. Brown Roux differs from white Roux mainly in color! All this must be done slowly, preferably in a heavy **iron** skillet over medium heat, stirring constantly until the desired color is obtained.

When this is done, lower the heat. (Turning on the air-conditioner is a reliable method.) Be sure the vegetables and other ingredients used in the recipe are added very slowly, and Violà, Roux!

SOME TIPS ON CREOLE COOKERY

1. When adding chopped vegetables, e.g. onion, bell pepper and celery to a Roux, let them cook slowly until soft or pulp-like—not brown—but 'wilted'.

2. Always add **hot** water to food—and do it slowly.

3. After hot water is added to a Roux and ingredients, simmer gently to preserve flavors and food value.

4. Never over-cook parsley but add it to simmering food about 3 minutes before serving time, otherwise the flavor is lost in over-cooking.

5. When making a tomato gravy, always add paprika to oil or fat in which you fry the onions. It adds flavor and enhances the color.

6. In meat cookery, brown meat on all sides in very hot fat or oil, then cook slowly with very low heat, thus preserving tenderness and juices with less shrinkage.

7. The pungent flavor of red onions are preferred by Southern cooks.

8. To simplify creole cookery, chop and prepare all seasonings before starting to cook. It makes things much easier. My daughter-in-law once remarked, "Mother, you do it all so smoothly!" To which I answered, "And why not, I've been getting things ready for an **hour!**" Then I hit her with a skillet (heavy iron is best for this)!

mother's favorite recipes

JAMBALAYA

'Jambalaya' is a famous Creole dish, with rice as the basic ingredient. Rice may be obtained from rice growers and most Oriental countries, but we've found that one of the best places to obtain rice is the grocery store. The dictionary says that the origin of the word 'Jambalaya' is uncertain, but intensive research on our part revealed the following.

Many years ago, a fat cook on a large plantation announced that he had discovered a new delicacy, using his own secret recipe. Upon hearing this, one of his neighbors, with whom he was not on the best of terms, exclaimed, "You Jumbo Liar!" (or large prevaricator). The news quickly spread through the plantation and from that day forward the cook was known as "Jumbo Liar"—a name that stuck like okra.

In later years the name was shortened to "Jambalaya (which in fact is the same length) and became synonymous with the recipe he had discovered. Thus the name "Jambalaya"!

SHRIMP JAMBALAYA

2 Cups Minute Rice
1 Lb. Shrimp, Devein & Cut In Pieces
1 Large Onion, Chopped
1 Cup Celery, Chopped
1 Can Tomato Sauce
1 Bell Pepper, Chopped
1 Tsp. Paprika
1 Tblsp. Green Onion Tops
1 Tblsp. Minced Parsley
2 Tblsp. Cooking Oil or Fat
3-4 Drops Tabasco Sauce
1 Sprig Thyme
1 Bayleaf
Garlic Salt To Taste

Heat oil & paprika until color deepens. Add chopped onions and celery, fry until tender (not brown). Add tomato sauce and other seasonings, add 1 cup hot water & cook 5 minutes, then add shrimp. Cook until shrimp are tender—not more than 10 minutes. Lift out bayleaf & thyme. Remove from fire and measure liquid accurately (cooked liquid must be measured to determine amount of hot water needed to steam Minute Rice. Check package for directions). Add required additional amount of hot water to cooked mixture; add rice, mixing thoroughly, add parsley and green onion tops. Place over low heat until it comes to a boil. Remove from fire, cover, and let stand for 6 minutes. Lift cover & mix gently. Serves six.

Oyster Jambalaya can be made the same way, except that you must use oysters instead of shrimp!

HAM & SAUSAGE JAMBALAYA

This recipe makes use of two of the pig's finer qualities, ham and sausage. The pig is described as a swine, wild or domestic. This means some are having a ball, while others have married and settled down. The pig may also be used in a derogatory manner, such as: "You, sir, are a swine!" To which he may answer, "And you, madam, are a pig!" The skin of the pig is mistakenly used to make footballs.

2 Cups Minute Rice	3 Tblsp. Butter
12 Sausages, Cut In Pieces	1 Tblsp. All-Purpose Flour
1 Slice Ham, Chopped	3 Finger Pinch Of Oregano
1 Large Onion, Chopped	1 Tblsp. Worcestershire
½ Cup Celery, Chopped	Sauce
6 Green Onions, Chopped	2 Tblsp. Parsley, Minced
2 Pods Garlic, Minced	Pepper Sauce To Taste

Fry cut sausages in small skillet. Set aside.

Heat 3 tblsp. butter, add sausage drippings; when hot, add flour, making a roux, stirring until light brown. Add onions, celery, minced garlic, ham, cooked sausage, oregano and let all cook until tender —about 10 minutes, stirring constantly. Add green onions, pepper sauce, Worcestershire sauce and parsley last. Salt to taste.

Follow Minute Rice directions for amount of boiling water needed. Add water and rice to mixture & let come to a boil. Stir thoroughly, cover, remove from fire and let stand 6 minutes before removing cover. Mix again before serving. (Serves 6).

CREOLE SEAFOOD 'SALAD'

1 Lb. Small Shrimp	2 Tsp. Lemon Juice
1 Small Can Crabmeat	1/8 Tsp. Kitchen Seasoning
1 Cup Boiled Ham	Salt & Pepper
(thick slice, diced)	Lettuce Leaves
2 Tblsp. Gr. Onion Tops,	1 1/2 Cups Minute Rice,
Finely Chopped	Cooked In Shrimp Broth
1/2 Cup Salad Dressing	

 ## SEASONING FOR SHRIMP BROTH

2 Celery Sticks	1 Lemon Wedge
1/2 Onion, Quartered	Salt To Taste
1 Bayleaf	

Boil shrimp, peel & devein. Cook Minute Rice in shrimp broth (in place of water) per directions on pkg. When rice is **cold,** loosen with fork and lightly mix in crabmeat, shrimp & diced ham. Then mix in all other seasonings & salad dressing. Serve on lettuce leaves garnished with sprigs of parsley as main luncheon dish or as entree. Delicious with crisp heated rolls.

BAKED STUFFED TOMATOES
(au Creole)

The tomato is a South American perennial herb which is widely cultivated as a fruit (like my cousin Percy). It is a rounded or oblate, pulpy berry which is red or yellow when ripe, and is served raw, as in salads, or cooked as a vegetable. Tomatoes also come in juice, ketchup, paste, pulp, puree, hampers and cans—and sometimes never! In this case they come stuffed.

4 Med. Tomatoes	2 Tsp. Lea & Perrin Sauce
½ Lb. Ground Pork & Beef	3 Drops Tabasco (to taste)
	1 Tblsp. Parsley, Minced
3 Tblsp. Butter	3 Tblsp. Toasted Crumbs
1 Med. Onion, Chopped	Parmesan Cheese
3 Cups Stale White Bread (squeezed very dry)	Salt to Taste

Cut slice off top of each tomato and scoop out pulp, being careful not to damage tomato 'cups'. Chop tomato pulp. Heat butter in iron skillet (med. heat) and brown meat with onion. Remove from fire. In same skillet, toss in squeezed bread, add more butter if needed and fry to golden brown. Add tomato pulp, browned meat, mixing until well blended, then add parsley, salt and sauces. Mix well. Fill tomato cups with meat mixture—place in baking pan, sprinkle with parmesan cheese and toasted crumbs—dot with butter—bake about 20 minutes in 350° oven, or until tomatoes are soft.

RED BEANS AND RICE

The once lowly red bean has risen to become one of the most famous delicacies of the South. Chock full of nutrition, it became the mainstay meal of a great many families during the depression, mainly because of its low price. For 15c you could buy enough red beans and rice, with a piece of pickled pork thrown in for lagniappe, to feed a family of 6. (This practice left many families of 5 or 7 without food!) Today, red beans and rice is on the menu of famous restaurants, not-so-famous restaurants, and almost every home in New Orleans. So give yourself a treat and whomp up a batch—here's the recipe.

1 Lb. Red Beans	2 Pods Garlic, Chopped Fine
1 ½" Slice Slab Bacon	1 Tblsp. Parsley
1 Large Onion, Chopped	1 Tblsp. Flour
1 Tblsp. Shortening	

Wash and pick over beans then place in 1½ qts. cold water over medium heat. Add slice of bacon, lower heat when it boils and cook until beans are tender, then remove from heat. Heat shortening and add flour, onions and garlic—fry until soft, not brown. Add mixture to beans, let cook over low heat. Add parsley and stir well until creamy. If too thick, add a little water.

Serve with steamed rice, and ham, smoked sausage, pork chops, or pickled pork if you live in the Deep South.

POTATO SALAD—a la MOTHER ROUX

The potato is a tuber plant
It's origin Peruvian.
So many recipes exist,
This one is 'Mother Rouxvian'!

6 Med. Sized Potatoes
2 Cups Celery, Chopped
2 Pods Pimentos, Chopped
4 Hard Boiled Eggs, Diced
2 Tblsp. Parsley, Finely
   Minced
2 Doz. Stuffed Olives,
   Sliced

Paprika & White Pepper to
   Taste
½ Cup Mayonnaise
1 Lemon, juice of which is
   added to Mayonnaise
1 Tblsp. Prep. Hot Mustard
1 Tblsp. Olive Oil
1 Tblsp. Vinegar

Boil potatoes in jackets. Let cool—peel and cut into thick slices, salting while warm.

Use large bowl. Add all dry ingredients to the cut potatoes—toss gently while mixing—add mayonnaise mixture, paprika and pepper. Add olive oil and vinegar last. Taste for salt content, add more if needed. For more tart taste, add more vinegar.

"MOTHER'S" MEAT BALLS

One morning, about 40 years ago, "Mother" was making a meat loaf from ground meat. Being a little tipsy from repeated nips at the cooking sherry, "Mother" kept dropping bits of meat on the floor. She noticed this (after stepping on a few) and, being the fastidious person that she is, asked the children to pick them up. While doing this the children rolled the flat pieces into little balls so they could be picked up easier. "Mother" popped them in with the rest of the meat muttering, "the fire will kill the germs," or "what they don't know won't hurt 'em," or words to that effect. As it happened they turned out very tasty and soon became one of "Mother's" favorite recipes.

MEAT RECIPE

2 Lbs. Ground Chuck
2 Eggs, Beaten
2 Tblsp. Ketchup
1 Pinch Oregano
1 Tblsp. Worcestershire
3 Tblsp. Oil
½ Tsp. Garlic Powder
⅔ Cup Bread Crumbs
Pepper Sauce

GRAVY RECIPE

2 Large Onions, Chopped
1 Can Stewed Tomatoes, Chopped
1 Bell Pepper, Chopped
½ Cup Celery, Chopped
1 Tblsp. Flour, Plain
2 Bayleaves
1 Cup Hot Water
Pepper Sauce

3 Tblsp. Parsley, Minced
½ Tblsp. Kitchen Seasoning
1 Tblsp. Paprika-Oregano
1 Tblsp. Worcestershire
Salt

Place meat in suitable sized bowl for mixing. Beat 2 large eggs in small bowl, add all seasoning. Pour egg mixture and mix **thoroughly** with your hands (best kitchen implement ever devised), sprinkle in bread crumbs and mix again, then lightly roll into 1½" yummy balls (makes about 16-18). Brown meat balls in hot oil, then place in large **warm** pot until gravy is made.

Gravy: Use drippings from meat balls, add more oil if necessary. Heat oil in heavy skillet and add flour, making a roux, stirring constantly until it's a golden brown. Lower heat, add paprika, onions, celery and bell pepper, mixing and stirring until very soft —about 10 minutes. Add tomatoes and other seasoning (except parsley) and cook over low heat ½ hour, stirring to prevent sticking (it sho 'nuff will stick if you don't). Add about a cup of hot water, or more if still too thick. Pour gravy over meat balls, simmer ½ hour, then add parsley. Boil gently 2 minutes and remove from heat.

Serve with spaghetti, generously sprinkled with parmesan cheese and a salad of grated carrots, shredded lettuce, diced dill pickle and your favorite salad dressing. Terrific!

CHEESE SOUFFLE

A souffle is a delicious, spongy, hot dish prepared from a savory mixture, usually containing minced cheese, fruit, fish, or meat, into which stiffly beaten egg whites have been folded—and is puffed by cooking. It is derived from the French 'souffle—to puff'. Cheese is a 'curd of milk used as an article of food'. Enough said about that!

6 Slices White Bread
   Cut Off Crust
	1 Cup Sharp Cheese,
	   Grated

3 Eggs	Butter and Salt
1½ Cups Milk	

Butter both sides of bread, cut into small pieces (about 9). Beat eggs well, add milk gradually. Butter casserole well. Start with bread, end with cheese; pour eggs and milk over bread and cheese. Soak 4 hours. Bake in 350° oven for one hour, with casserole in pan of water. Easy to fix, especially if it is put together a day ahead (what isn't?). This one will surprise you—its' terrific! It will souffle you (puff you up)!

BEEF VEGETABLE SOUP SUPREME

5-6 Shin Marrow Bones, Strip Meat
2 Lbs. Heavy Beef Chuck
1 Lb. Beef Brisket
1 Can Tomato Sauce
2 Tblsp. Vinegar
1 Small Can Tomatoes, Chopped
4-5 Carrots, Diced
2 Potatoes, Peeled and Diced
3 Cups Cabbage, Shredded
4 Cups Celery, Chopped
1 Large Onion, Chopped
1 Cup String Beans, Cut
⅓ Cup Parsley, Minced
1 Cup Vermicelli, Crumbled

Put shin bones on to boil, using a 6 qt. kettle with 1 gallon of water, making sure the water comes all the way up to your knees. Add tomato sauce and vinegar. It is said that the acid in the tomatoes and vinegar draws the calcium, which we all need, from the bones. (This statement was made by Dr. Pierre La Toole, who is no longer allowed to practice medicine in Louisiana). Boil bones for 3 hours over low heat (or until they start to rattle), then add meat and brisket. When broth returns to boiling point, skim off film, and take a couple snapshots of the soup. Boil meat for 2 hours (low heat), then remove bones and add marrow to boiling soup. Add tomatoes and all vegetables and simmer for 1 hour, or until vegetables are cooked. Add vermicelli and minced parsley and cook a few minutes more.

This soup will make your mouth water!

seafood

SHRIMP REMOULADE

Many years ago there lived a chicken named "Remmo" which, after being fed an original concoction by her owner, would lay a tremendous egg! One day after her meal she laid an egg of such huge dimensions that it caused her owner's son to loudly exclaim, "Dad! Come see what Remmo laid!" Her owner began attributing her huge success in the reproductive department to the special formula he had been feeding her, and, because his son (who wasn't too bright) would invariably shout, "Remmo laid! Remmo laid! "everytime Remmo laid a big egg, he soon began calling his recipe "Remmo Laid." When the French came to Louisiana "Remmo Laid" was given the French spelling and pronunciation. Thus "Remoulade" was born!

1 Lb. Shrimp, Fresh or Frozen	Juice Of ½ Lemon
3 Tblsp. Olive or Salad Oil	1 Tblsp. Vinegar
2 Hard Boiled Eggs	2 Tblsp. Mustard With Horse-Radish
¼ Teasp. Paprika	2 tblsp. Celery Hearts, Minced
Garlic Salt	Shredded Lettuce

Boil shrimp in salted water. Peel and devein. Mash egg yolks. Place other ingredients in bowl, mix thoroughly with fork—add yolks—add cooked shrimp. Mix thoroughly so that each shrimp is well coated. Refrigerate at least 2-3 hours.

Serve small portion on lettuce as appetizer before dinner. Serves six.

SHRIMP CREOLE

Shrimp Creole is a favorite around these parts. Louisiana is noted for its abundance of shrimp **and** Creoles, so it was quite natural that the two got together. (Some say that "Shrimp Creole" was a very short Frenchman, but we can find nothing to authenticate this.)

2 Lbs. Shrimp	1 Large Can Stewed
2 Tblsp. Olive Oil	Tomatoes, Chopped
2 Tblsp. Bacon Drippings	¼ Tsp. Oregano
1 Large Bell Pepper,	2 Tbsp. Parsley, Minced
Chopped	1 Tsp. Sugar
1 Cup Onions, Chopped	3-4 Slices Lemon
1 Cup Celery, Chopped	

Peel shrimp and devein. Set aside. Heat oil and bacon drippings in a heavy skillet. Add onions, pepper, celery and cook until soft. Add tomato pulp and lemon and let simmer (covered) for about ½ hour, stirring occasionally. Add oregano, sugar, shrimp and enough tomato liquid so the gravy will cover the shrimp. Add hot water if necessary. Let shrimp cook until tender and add parsley. Serve with steamed dry rice.

FISH COURTBOUILLON

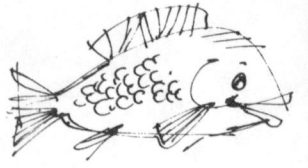

We all know what fish is (especially if its been in the sun for a few days). Court Bouillon is another matter. We looked into it and found that Court means to make love, to woo; as to go courting. Bouillon, on the other hand, is a clear stock made by boiling beef or other things in water. Putting this information together, we gather that Courtbouillon (pronounced coo-bi-on) was discovered by a guy who made love to stock!

6 ½" Slices Fresh Fish	2 Cloves
2 Red Onions, Chopped Fine	1 Tsp. Paprika
	2 Pods Garlic, Chopped
2 Cups Stewed Tomatoes	2 Tblsp. Parsley, Minced
½ Cube Butter	4 Slices Lemon
½ Bell Pepper, Chopped	Tabasco Or Cayenne
2 Tblsp. Flour, Plain	Pepper (to taste)
2 Bay Leaves	Salt And Black Pepper

Season fish with salt & pepper, then refrigerate. Heat butter in skillet, add flour making a roux. Do not over-brown. Add paprika, then saute onions, bell pepper and garlic and cook 10 minutes. Add tomatoes, cloves, bayleaf, lemon slices and cook 5 minutes. Add 2 cups boiling water, then let all ingredients cook 30 minutes. **Gently** place fish (how can you be gentle to a dead fish?) in boiling gravy, using medium heat, and cooking until fish begins to flake, or 30 minutes **uncovered.** Then put your clothes back on and remove bayleaf and cloves. Add parsley and pepper sauce 3 minutes before serving. Serves six. Delicious with creamed potatoes and tossed salad.

BAKED RED FISH OR SNAPPER

Red fish abound in southern waters, and it is the only fish in the world that knows how to blush. If you happen to catch one while it's doing something bad, it will stay red forever—thus giving it the name 'Red' fish.

1 4 Lb. Red Fish (snapper)	2 Tblsp. Green Onions Minced
4 Very Ripe Fresh Tomatoes, Mashed	2 Tsp. Worcestershire
1 Cup Toasted Bread Crumbs	2 Tblsp. Butter
	1 Tblsp. Olive Oil
1 Lemon—½ For Juice ½ Thinly Sliced	2-3 Dashes Pwd. Thyme Pepper Sauce or Cayenne
2 Tblsp. Parsley, Minced	Salt

Prepare the following in suitable sized baking pan, making a "bed" for the fish (if fish falls asleep, shake gently):

Place olive oil in pan, then ½ of mashed tomatoes, ½ of bread crumbs; sprinkle 1 tblsp. of minced green onions and parsley, a little thyme, 1 tsp. Worcestershire sauce, sprinkle with lemon juice and dot with ½ of the butter. Lay the fish (salted & peppered) on this "bed." Repeat procedure on top of fish (if this doesn't wake him up, nothing will)—until a layer of ingredients cover the fish. Embed several slices of lemon in the ingredients in addition to lemon juice.

Bake in moderate oven—350° for ½ hour, adding 1 cup of water before placing in oven. Check at 25 minutes . . . if flesh of fish is white, it is cooked. Serve with buttered creamed potatoes, a mixed tossed salad and very crisp rolls. Fit for a King!

DIANE'S

CRABMEAT IMPERIAL

The crab is a most tasty member of the crustacean family that literally abounds in the warm, shallow waters of Louisiana. Crabs are prepared in a variety of delicious dishes and are literally caught and consumed by the ton. The crab possesses the dubious ability of being able to walk in any direction without turning, but usually prefers sideways—so he can see, not where he's going or where he's been, but what's on the other side. The crab has the distinction of being the zodiacal symbol for the sign of Cancer, and a crab is also an ill-tempered person, usually old (as in, 'you old crab, you'). Imperial is defined as 'royal or of superior excellence'—that's just what this is!

3 Lbs. Fresh Crabmeat	2 Eggs
1 Cup Mayonnaise	1 Tblsp. Dry Mustard
1 Bell Pepper, Chopped	1 Tsp. Salt
2 Pimento Pods, Chopped	1 Tsp. White Pepper

Beat eggs, mix in other ingredients, then fold (do not crease) in crabmeat.Sprinkle top with bread crumbs —dot with butter. Bake at 350° for about 40 minutes. Serves 8.

Note: After ingredients are mixed, don't worry about not having enough 'moisture' to handle the crabmeat. You will.

DEVILLED CRAB
(Gulf Coast Style)

Don't sit and pout—try this one out,
There's really nothing to it.
If asked just why—here's your reply,
"The devil made me do it!"

1 Lb. Crab Meat
1 Onion, Chopped
3 Hard Boiled Eggs,
    Mashed
2 Tblsp. Toasted Bread
    Crumbs

2 Tsp. Parsley, Minced
1 Tblsp.Worcestershire
    Sauce
1 Tblsp. Lemon Juice
¼ Tsp. Curry Powder

WHITE SAUCE RECIPE

3 Tblsp. Butter
2 Tblsp. Flour
1 Chicken Bouillon Cube

½ Tsp. Dry Mustard
Salt and Pepper
Few Dashes of Cayenne

Dissolve bouillon cube in one cup of boiling water. Make white sauce by heating butter in skillet, using **low heat;** then stir in flour gradually and slowly add bouillon, stirring constantly. When smooth, add mustard, salt and pepper and cayenne. Stir in crabmeat and remaining ingredients. Blend thoroughly. Place mixture in shallow pan, lightly greased. Top with crumbs and dot with butter. Bake 40 minutes at 325°.

TROUT ALMONDINE

The trout is described as any fish of the Salmonidae family, but are usually much smaller than the salmon. There are exceptions, however, since shrewd, old speckled trout have been landed in Louisiana weighing from 8 to 12 lbs. Trout usually travel in schools (learning as they go) and sometimes even allow themselves to be bussed from one neighborhood to another. The salt waters of the Gulf Coast teem with speckled and white trout, but the rainbow is usually caught in the cold mountain streams of the Northwest. The trout is highly esteemed by fishermen everywhere for its fine flavor, rich, firm flesh, handsome color and gameness. On occasion they have been heard to yell, "I'm game—how about you"?

2 Lbs. Tenderloined Trout	1 Small Can Almonds, Chopped
1 Cup All-purpose Flour	
¾ Cup Evaporated Milk	1 Tsp. Salt & Pepper
⅓ Cup Butter	A Few Dashes of Cayenne
2 Tblsp. Cooking Oil	4 Lemon Wedges
	A Few Sprigs Parsley

Season flour with salt, pepper and cayenne. Dip each piece of trout in milk, then roll in the well-seasoned flour until thickly coated. Heat butter and oil in heavy skillet and fry trout, uncovered, using high heat. When evenly browned on both sides, remove from skillet. Pour off ½ of drippings and saute the chopped almonds until crisp. Sprinkle almonds over fish— garnish with lemon wedges and parsley. Serve immediately, even if no one is there!

 # DEVILLED OYSTERS

The Devil, according to Christian and Jewish theology, is the personal supreme spirit of evil, the tempter and spiritual enemy of mankind, the adversary of God, a satyr-like demon possessing the powers of darkness and the supreme ruler of Heck! He is also an ex-angel, a part-time flamethrower and the father of Rosemary's baby, so if you eat these oysters, Heck knows what will happen to you!

1 Pt. Oysters	3 Gr. Onions, Chopped
6-8 Salter Crackers,	Fine
Crumbled	Parsley Flakes
Lee & Perrins Sauce	
Tabasco Sauce	

Drain oysters and chop fine. Saute onions, using some of the tops, in butter. Add oysters and Lee & Perrins and Tabasco to taste. Turn off fire—add cracker crumbs and mix lightly. Place in buttered casserole or individual shells, sprinkle with parsley flakes and dot with butter. Bake for 30 minutes at 350°. This may be prepared ahead and refrigerated.

SHRIMP, CRAB AND OKRA GUMBO

Gumbo is a soup thickened with the mucilaginous pods of okra. Mucilaginous means moist and viscid, or sticky. Okra is a vegetable cultivated in the southern United States and the West Indies for its mucilaginous green pods, used as the basis of soups, stews, etc. One dish prepared with this vegetable is gumbo. Now, in review, this dish seems to consist of shrimp, crabs, and various other ingredients all held together in one sticky mass by okra!

2 Lbs. Fresh Shrimp, Deveined	2 Stalks Celery, Chopped
2 Cans Crabmeat	2 Lbs. Okra, Sliced Thin
3 Slices Bacon, Crisped And Crumbled	¼ Cup Oil, Plus Bacon Drippings
2 Red Onions, Large, Chopped Fine	3 Tblsp. Flour
3-4 Green Onions, Chopped Fine	3 Tblsp. Tomato Paste
4 Pods Garlic, Minced	3 Tblsp. Parsley, Chopped
	2 Bayleaves
	Salt And Pepper Sauce
	3 Qts. Boiling Water

Chop all vegetables, etc. before starting to cook. Using heavy skillet, fry okra in bacon drippings, using medium heat, until it is dry and ropiness disappears —about ½ hour. In another heavy pot, brown flour in hot oil. When golden brown, add paprika, onions, celery and garlic, using low flame, and fry until well cooked, stirring constantly. Add tomato paste & cook a few more minutes.

In large pot containing 3 to 4 quarts of boiling water, add okra & all cooked ingredients to water along with bay leaves, green onions & hot pepper and let cook until okra is tender (½ hour). Add shrimp, crabmeat and bacon, using very low heat and stirring often. Simmer ½ hour. Salt and pepper to taste. Then add parsley and cook another 3 minutes. Serve in soup plate with steamed rice on the side.

OYSTERS ROCKEFELLER

John Z. Rockefeller was a great American philanthropist who was born in 1839, under the Sign of the Oyster. He developed an insatiable desire for oysters when, just before he was born, his Mother darted in front of an oyster wagon and was nearly done in. This gave him something in common with the oyster, since he felt like doing her in himself on numerous occasions. During his lifetime he devoured many an oyster, prepared every way imaginable, but the recipe that now bears his name, he loved the best!

6 Oysters per Serving	1 Bunch Parsley, Small
¼ Lb. Butter, Melted	1 Bunch Spinach, Small
½ Celery Stalk	1 Bunch Beet Tops, Small
1 Bunch Green Onion Tops	Juice of 1 or 2 Lemons

Fill appropriate number of pie plates with rock salt. Place 6 oysters on half shell in each pie plate. Grind all greens with celery, very fine, add melted butter and lemon juice. Place a teaspoonful on each oyster, place pie plates in broiler and cook rapidly until oysters curl. Serve right in the pie plates. Watch the table cloth—it might catch fire.

CRAYFISH ETOUFFEE (A-2-FAY)

Everyone knows what a Crayfish is. In some areas they are called Crawfish, in others Crawdads, and, in some sections of the South, they are lovingly referred to as 'Mudbugs'. Etouffee means 'to smother' in French. To prepare this recipe, you either must use a pan with a very tight lid, so that no air can get in, or hold a pillow firmly over the face of each Crayfish. The first method, we find, is much easier and doesn't bring that feeling of guilt.

1 Lb. Peeled Crayfish
  Tails, with Fat
¼ Lb. Butter
2 Med. Onions, Chopped
  Fine
1 Pod Garlic, Finely
  Minced
1 Large tblsp. Tomato
  Paste

2 Slices Lemon, Thin
1 Tblsp. Parsley, Chopped
1 Tblsp. Green Onion,
  Chopped
1 Tsp. Salt
¼ Tsp. Red Pepper
½ Tsp. Cornstarch, With
  3 tblsp. Water

Melt butter in saucepan with tight fitting lid, add onion and cook over medium low heat until tender, stirring constantly. Add tomato paste and garlic and cook about 5 minutes, stirring all the while. Combine the remaining ingredients and add to cooked mixture and cover. Raise heat, when it boils cook five minutes more. Serve over hot rice.

DES HUITE (OYSTERS)
in puff paste patty shells

The oyster is a marine bivalve mollusk of the genius Ostrea or family Ostreidae. It has an irregular shell which is closed by a single adductor muscle (and opened the same way, I suppose). They are found lying around the bottom in the shallow water of the seacoasts waiting for their food, which consists of minute plants & animals, to be carried to them by the current (that's lazy when they won't even go out for food). They are cultivated (which means you really have to get to know 'em) for food in many regions, such as here.

6 Patty Shells	1 Tblsp. Green Onion
1½ Doz. Oysters & Water	Tops, Chopped
2 Tblsp. Onions,	1 Tblsp. Parsley, Minced
Chopped	2 Tsp. Lemon Juice
2 Tblsp. Plain Flour	3-4 Drops Tabasco Sauce
4 Tblsp. Butter	1 Bayleaf, Small
⅓ Cup Celery, Minced	Salt and Hot Water

Pick over oysters for shell particles—save water. Heat butter in heavy skillet over medium heat and make roux by adding flour. Stir until golden brown, then add onions and celery and cook until soft, stirring constantly. Add green onions, bayleaf, lemon juice, Tabasco sauce and salt. Let cook 5 minutes, add oysters and oyster water and cook 4 to 5 minutes. If too thick, add a little boiling water. Oyster mixture must be **very thick.** Remove bayleaf.

Place patty shells in shallow pan, remove tops from shells and spoon 3 oysters and portion of thick sauce into each shell. Replace tops and bake in 350° oven until shells are crisp, usually about 15-20 minutes. Place on warm platter & garnish with crisp parsley. Always serve before entree.

CRAB MEAT IN AVOCADO HALVES

The Crab leads an unhappy life,
He has no fun, he takes no wife,
His future's grim—no chance to laugh,
He ends up in an avocado half!

2 Ripe Avocados
½ Can Crab Meat
3 Hard Boiled Eggs,
   Mashed
1 Small Dill Pickle,
   Chopped

½ Cup Mayonnaise
½ Lemon (juice of)
   Tabasco Sauce, to Taste
   Salt & Black Pepper,
      to Taste

Scoop out about ½ of avocado pulp—mash and sprinkle on lemon juice to prevent discoloring. Place all ingredients in bowl together with mashed avocado, toss lightly (not quite to ceiling), and spoon into avocado shells. Place each half on lettuce and serve before entree. Or serve as luncheon snack with salted crackers or thins (not Virginia). Serves 4, because each avocado has 2 halves.

meat & poultry

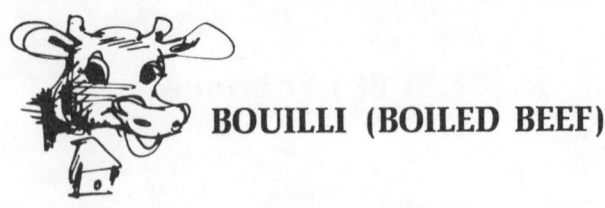

BOUILLI (BOILED BEEF)

Bouilli, or boiled beef, was discovered by a New Englander named Bouilli, who had nothing to cook his meat in except water. In fact, he cooked everything in water and, unknown to him, he originated the New England boiled dinner. "Mother" glommed onto this recipe while touring Martha's Vineyard in search of Martha. She didn't find Martha but she did run into Bouilli, who in a tender moment of gratitude, gave her this recipe!

3 Lbs. Short Ribs of Beef Lean, in Serving Pieces	3 Celery Branches, Cut into 1" Lengths
1 Large Onion, Quartered	2 Tsp. Salt
4 Med. Carrots, Scraped	4 Sprigs Parsley
4 Med. Potatoes	3 Qts. Boiling Water

HORSE-RADISH SAUCE

1 Tblsp. Horse-Radish	1 Tsp. Lemon Juice
¾ Cup Ketchup	Salt

Mix ingredients for sauce and refrigerate. When water boils add meat, celery, onions, carrots, parsley and salt. When it returns to boiling point, lower heat and boil gently until meat is **very tender,** at least 2 hours or more. Add potatoes during last hour. When cooked, remove bones and parsley—serve with horse-radish sauce and vegetables. Remaining broth may be used in gravies or added to soup.

P.S. Bouilli is served in many New Orleans French restaurants . . . so try it!

BEEF DAUBE au Carrotte

'Daube' (pronounced dobe) literally means to stew meat in a sauce, or, larded meat braised with vegetables. It was originated about 1800 by a meat-loving gourmet known as the Earl of Daube, who also originated adobe haciendas and Daube (later called Dobey) Gillis. Here is his recipe.

3 Lbs. Beef Shoulder	2 Tsp. Horse-Radish
2 Large Onions, Chopped	Mustard
2 Cans Tomato Paste	2 Cups Celery, Chopped
1 Can Tomato Sauce	3 Pods Garlic
1 Large Bell Pepper	2 Sprigs Thyme
3 Tblsp. All-Purpose Flour	6 Carrots, Cut Length-Wise
3 Tblsp. Cooking Oil	Hot Water
	Salt

Make small slits in meat with pointed knife and insert slivers of garlic (1 pod). Heat oil in heavy pot, brown meat on all sides and set aside, keeping it warm. Into meat drippings add flour and brown lightly, stirring constantly. Add onions, bell pepper, celery and crushed garlic and let cook till pulpy. Add tomato paste and sauce and cook 5 minutes. Add about 3 cups hot water, mix and let simmer. Replace meat in pot so that it is covered by liquid. Then lower heat and add thyme. Cover tightly, simmer about 1 hour. Add carrots and cook until meat and carrots are tender. Add parsley and cook 2 minutes. Serves six.

Serve with macaroni topped generously with sharp cheddar cheese.

ROAST PIQUANT—CAJUN STYLE

A roast is a hunk of meat. Piquant means agreeably stimulating to the taste, pleasantly tart, sharp, etc. A Cajun is a person of Acadian (thus the name Cajun) French descent who left Acadia, which was the original name for Nova Scotia, in 1755 and eventually settled in south Louisiana, bringing with them many culinary mysteries, one of which is their recipe for dry-marinating a roast. Here it is.

4 Lb. Beef Roast (approx.)	1 Tblsp. Paprika
1 Tsp. Black Pepper	2 Tblsp. Table Seasoning
2 Tsp. Garlic Salt	1 Tblsp. Hot Mustard

Blend all ingredients and firmly rub into all sides of the roast. Place roast in suitable sized pan or pot and cover air-tight. Refrigerate at least 12 hours before cooking.

Roast until tender, basting often.

PORK CHOPS—SOUTHERN STYLE
(serve with minted apple jelly)

Pork chops, southern style, are not by any means to be confused with pork chops, northern style. Our research department found that these two dishes originated some time ago when a pig happened to be standing directly on the Mason-Dixon line. Two families claimed the pig, one from the north, the other from the south. To settle their dispute they agreed to cut the pig in half—right down the line! Both halves of the pig contained pork chops, but the best our research department could come up with was the **southern** recipe. Here it is, you all.

4 **Pork Chops, ¾" Thick**	2 **Tblsp. Drippings Or**
2 **Tblsp. Flour, Approx.**	**Cooking Oil**
1 **Cup Hot Milk**	**Salt & Freshly Ground**
	Black Pepper

To make sauce, crush 2 tsp. mint leaves and mince finely. Stir into 1 cup of apple jelly, then refrigerate.

Trim pork chops, season with salt and pepper, then roll in flour. Brush the flour off you, then heat drippings in heavy skillet and brown pork chops, using medium heat. Remove chops and place in shallow baking pan. Brown remaining flour in drippings, using same skillet, then **slowly** add the hot milk. Stir until it thickens. Season to taste and pour over chops. Bake in 375° oven about 45 minutes. Serves 4.

Serve with creamed potatoes to which 2 or 3 dashes of nutmeg has been added—and don't forget the mint sauce in the refrigerator!

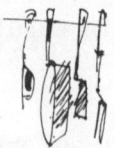

PIMENTO MEAT LOAF

A juicy, tempting, tasty dish
A meat loaf is all one could wish.
While leaving all the jokes behind,
"Don't let your meat loaf", comes to mind!

1½ Lbs. Ground Beef
    (lean)
½ Lb. Pork Sausage
2 Large Pimentos,
    Chopped
3 Tblsp. Onions, Minced
2 Eggs, Well Beaten
3 Tblsp. Ketchup

1 Tblsp. Worcestershire
1 Cup Quick Oatmeal
    (crumbled) or Corn
    Flake Crumbs
1 Tsp. Salt
1 Tsp. Prep. Mustard
⅛ Tsp. Oregano
    Cold Water

Mix all ingredients, adding just enough cold water to mix thoroughly. Use scant tsp. of salt if sausage is seasoned. Add beaten eggs and then mix thoroughly. Pack into well-greased loaf pan (or ungreased suitcase) and bake in moderate oven at 350° for 1¼ hours. Serve 6 generously. If there are only 2 in your family, invite Bob and Carol and Ted and Alice over for dinner!

VEAL STEAKS—SPANISH STYLE

One day Don Pablo Cortez came home after a hard days work and asked his wife what was cooking for supper. When she replied, "Chili and beans," he flew into a rage, pulled his gun and took a shot at her screaming, "Chili and beans, chili and beans, everyday, chili and beans! Can't you cook anything else, woman?" Fortunately, his shot missed his wife and hit a calf that was frolicking in the kitchen. His wife sobbed, "I have nothing else to cook—can you think of something?" He snarled, "you've got a dead calf right there— don't waste it, woman! How about veal steaks, Spanish style?"

She prepared them according to this recipe, making Don Pablo very happy.

2 Veal Rounds	1 Pod Garlic, Crushed
2 Tblsp. Olive Oil	¼ Tsp. Oregano
1½ Cups Bread Crumbs	1 Tblsp. Green Onion Tops,
1 Large Egg	Minced
2 Tblsp. Vinegar	Cayenne Pepper to Taste

Cut veal rounds into several pieces. Beat egg and vinegar, oregano and garlic pod. Mix bread crumbs with salt and plenty of black and cayenne pepper. Spread crumb mixture on waxed paper, then dip each piece of veal in egg and seasoned crumbs. Fry in hot oil until brown and drain on paper towel. Serve on hot platter garnished with sprigs of parsley. Sprinkle with parmesan cheese.

Serve with stewed eggplant, Spanish style.

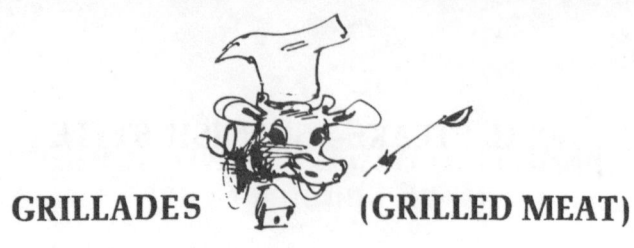

GRILLADES (GRILLED MEAT)

1 Beef Round ½ Thick	2 Tblsp. Flour
1 Cup Onions, Chopped	3 Tblsp. Cooking Oil
½ Can Tomato Paste	1 Sprig Thyme
1 Cup Tomatoes	2 Pods Garlic
2 Bouillon Cubes	Minced Parsley
	Salt

Dissolve 2 beef bouillon cubes in 1½ cups of boiling water and save. Cut round into serving pieces and brown quickly in oil using heavy pot. When meat is grilled, remove from pot and set aside (making sure not to lose it in the confusion). Add onions, garlic and flour to meat drippings and stir until light brown. Slowly add tomato paste and tomatoes, stirring constantly. Let cook 5 minutes then slowly add the 1½ cups beef bouillon and stir. Add grilled meat, cover closely, lower heat and simmer until meat is very tender, about 45 minutes to an hour, depending upon the age of the meat (be sure to ask the butcher how old the cow was). Add parsley and cook 2 or 3 minutes.

Serve with rice or with ham and sausage jambalaya —or serve it with gusto. Or just throw it in the freezer and trot on over to Colonel Sanders!

BRAISED CALF LIVER AND ONIONS
(With Buttered Grits)

1 Lb. Calf Liver (sliced)	3 Tblsp. Butter
3 Onions, Rings	1 Tblsp. Lemon Juice
2 Pods, Garlic, Minced	1 Tblsp. Worcestershire
3 Tblsp. Flour	Pinch of Oregano
Hot Water	Salt & Pepper

Remove skin (and sit around in your bones) and tubes from liver. Spread flour on waxed paper and coat each slice of liver thoroughly. Set aside (left). Heat butter in heavy skillet over medium heat, add liver slices (if your answer is 6, add them again) and cook slowly over low heat, turning several times until you're facing the stove. (If you turn too often, people will think you are either dancing or weird). When cooked, remove from skillet. Into drippings add onions, garlic and oregano—add more butter if needed—cooking until onions are soft, not brown. Add lemon juice, Worcestershire sauce and about ½ cup of hot water. Add liver and cook about 5 minutes using **very low heat.** Salt & pepper to taste. Overcooking and premature salting will toughen liver. (My uncle Fargo had a tough liver and he had a terrible time)!

Cook grits as per directions on package. Add 2 tblsp. butter and serve very hot. Liver and grits are strictly from the Deep South. Thumb lickin' good!

BEEFED-UP CHILI & CHEESE
(On Fritos)

If he likes food a little bit spicy,
From south of the border, that is,
Try this one on your 'caballero',
He'll say, "Golly, oh Heavens, gee whiz!"

2 Lbs. Round Steak,
   Ground
1 Tblsp. Fat
2 Pods Garlic, Minced
1 #2 Can Tomato Juice
1 Lb. Sharp Cheese,
   Grated

2 Med. Onions, Chopped
Chili Powder (Gebhardt's
   is good)
A Little Flour
Brick of Frozen Chili
Large Head of Lettuce
Fritos

Place ground steak in heavy skillet with fat over very low fire and stir until it is brown. Add garlic. Sift a **little** flour over this to take up the juice—add tomato juice and one cup of cold water. Let it cook and thicken—add chili powder, a little at a time. Taste now, because it gets **hot** quick-like. Add the frozen chili. Let this cook over low heat for one hour. Remove from heat—re-heat before serving. Pour meat sauce over a good serving of Fritos, add grated cheese and chopped onions. Cover with shredded lettuce. Serves 6.

NOTE: Here's a little secret between us girls—this may be prepared a day ahead and reheated. I won't tell if you don't!

CHICKEN FRICASSEE—PLANTATION STYLE
(with Dumplings)

Fricassee is described as a dish made of fowl or other meat of small animals (no sneaking in any elephant or giraffe, now—gopher is especially good, and is permissible) cut into pieces and stewed in gravy. (Personally, I'd rather get stewed in a bar)!

1 Young Hen	1 Bell Pepper, Chopped
2 Large Onions, Chopped	2 Sprigs Thyme
2 Tblsp. Oil	2 Tblsp. Parsley, Chopped
2 Tblsp. Butter	5-6 Drops Tabasco
3 Tblsp. Flour, Plain	Salt & Pepper to Taste
2 Tblsp. Green Onion Tops	Render Chicken Fat to
3 Pods Garlic, Minced	Use Drippings

Cut young hen (check birth certificate) into several pieces and brown in butter over low heat in heavy pot. Remove from pot and set aside, keeping warm (put on a coat if necessary). Brown flour in hot oil and drippings. When medium brown, add onions, garlic and bell pepper, stirring constantly. Cook until tender, then slowly add 3 cups boiling water—stir—add chicken pieces (large pieces on the bottom). Add thyme, salt, pepper and simmer until chicken is tender. Add parsley 3 minutes before serving. Serve with steamed rice, a green salad and **dumplings.**

Note: You couldn't make better dumplings than to follow the recipe on a Bisquick package—2 cups Bisquick, ¾ cup milk and mix with fork. Teaspoon into boiling gravy. Cook over low heat for 10 minutes uncovered and then 10 minutes tightly covered. Makes 10 to 12 dumplings.

BAKED SPRING CHICKEN OR CORNISH HEN
(Served with Banana Fritters)

1 2 Lb. Fryer, Cut in Half	Paprika
3 Tblsp. Melted Butter	Salt and Pepper
1 Pinch Oregano,	Lemon Juice
Crumbled on Each Half	Cooking Oil

To prepare chicken for baking (talk to it—make it understand that this is for it's own good), sprinkle with lemon juice and rub **inside** with piece of lemon (paying particular attention to the underarms). Crawl out, and sprinkle with salt, pepper and a few dashes of paprika. Spread with melted butter and then with crumbled oregano. Place in greased baking pan, breast side up (never lay chicken on its breast—this hurts and may produce breast cancer) in 400° oven for 15 minutes. Baste with melted butter and lower temperature to 300° until cooked, about 1 hour. Delicious with Banana Fritters. See next page.

NOTE: If Cornish hen is used, have butcher saw it in half length-wise while frozen. Then allow butcher to thaw. Another method is to insert a large firecracker into the hen's nether opening and blow it apart!

BANANA FRITTERS

1 Cup All Purpose Flour	½ Cup Milk
1 Large Egg	2 Tblsp. Melted Butter
1 Tsp. Baking Powder	2 Small Bananas, Mashed
1 Tsp. Sugar	¼ Tsp. Nutmeg

If you have a bunch of lazy bananas that just fritter their time away, this will teach them a lesson!

Sift flour, baking powder and salt together. Beat egg in bowl, because if you don't use a bowl, it splatters up the whole kitchen. Add other ingredients. Mash (from the picture of the same name) bananas with a few drops of lemon juice, add to batter, beating thoroughly, using a large banana whip. Drop by scant teaspoonsful into deep, hot oil (about 4 feet ought to do it), and fry 3 to 4 minutes until brown. Do not crowd fritters while frying (if anything a fritter hates, it's to be crowded). Drain on paper towels.

Delicious with Baked Spring Chicken or Cornish Hen (sawed lengthwise by a frozen butcher).

CHICKEN BREASTS WITH
APRICOTS & NUTMEG

4 Chicken Breasts	Lemon Wedge
1 Cup Apricots, Dried	Nutmeg
2 Tblsp. Butter	Salt

Soak 1 cup of apricots in warm water for several hours, then puree in blender or run through sieve. After you have run through sieve, try to pull yourself together. Rub each chicken breast on both sides (until it gets a dreamy look in its eyes) with lemon wedge. Sprinkle with salt and spread with butter. Wrap separately in aluminum foil and place in shallow pan. Bake at 375° for 30 minutes. Unwrap each breast, baring them to the public, and spread with pureed apricots and a few dashes of nutmeg. (If that doesn't attract attention, nothing will!) Bake for another 30 minutes, then open foil and run under broiler to brown quickly (or put on some suntan oil and go out to the beach like everybody else).

Serve with parslied potatoes or French fries. Serves 4, sensuously!

CREOLE CHICKEN FILÉ GUMBO

Creole chickens differ from other chickens mainly in the way they are fed. The Creoles feed them file powder, thyme, bay leaf, garlic, onions and parsley. This gives them heartburn and makes them rather mean, and, on occasion, they have been known to attack cats, dogs, and even small livestock upon the slightest provocation. They lay very spicy eggs!

1 Chicken (hen)	3 Tblsp. Oil
2 Red Onions	2 Sprigs Thyme
½ Cup Celery, Chopped	1 Bay Leaf
2 Pods Garlic, Chopped	1 Tblsp. Filé Powder
1 Small Bell Pepper, Chpd	(or more—to taste)
5 Green Onions, Chopped	3-4 Drops Tabasco
½ Can Tomato Paste	1 Tsp. Poultry Seasoning
3 Tblsp. Parsley, Chopped	Salt & Pepper to Taste
Several Sprigs Parsley	1 Wedge Lemon
3 Tblsp. Flour, Plain	

Filé is a powdered herb made from dried leaves of the sassafras tree. It has an aromatic, pungent flavor. Caution: NEVER boil filé powder—add it to gumbo after removing from fire.

Cut up chicken and boil until **not quite tender** in water containing chopped celery, parsley sprigs, poultry seasoning, lemon wedge and garlic pod. Let cool and strip meat from bones and cut into bit-sized pieces. Strain liquid and save for gumbo.

GUMBO: Heat oil (and bacon drippings if available) in heavy pot; add flour and stir constantly, making medium brown roux. Add onions and other chopped vegetables, tomato paste—cook until tender. Put chicken broth and enough hot water to make 4 qts. in a large pot. Boil broth-water then add mixture and chicken. Lower fire and simmer an hour. Add chopped parsley and green onions—cook 5 minutes more—remove from fire and sprinkle filé powder into gumbo and stir vigorously. Serve in soup plate with rice.

OVEN-FRIED CHICKEN

1 2½ to 3 Lb. Spring
   Chicken
½ Cup Evaporated Milk
1 Cup Seasoned Bread
   Crumbs

1 Pod Garlic, Crushed
⅛ Tsp. Crumbled Oregano
1 Tsp. Paprika
1 Lemon Wedge

Rub chicken inside and out with lemon wedge, which ought to just about cover everywhere! Add crushed garlic to evaporated milk (and watch it gag). Cut chicken into frying pieces and dry thoroughly. Dip each piece in evaporated milk, then roll in bread crumbs (screaming and kicking your feet as you do so). Place chicken in foil-lined pan without crowding, placing large pieces toward back of pan, where they can't get out! Bake at 350° for 20 minutes, then reduce heat to 300° for 35 to 45 minutes, depending on the size of chicken. Delicious with buttered creamed potatoes to which a few dashes of nutmeg have been added.

NOTE: Instead of bread crumbs, you might try Corn Flake Crumbs, which gives a crisp coating to chicken and smells better than burnt feathers. To 1 cup of Corn Flake Crumbs, add 1 tsp. salt, ⅛ tsp. black pepper, a few flecks of cayenne and ⅛ tsp. grated nutmeg and proceed as above.

CHICKEN PIQUANT—WITH PETIT POIS

Chicken Piquant differs from Chicken Creole mainly in conduct—they are not quite so vicious! Intensive research reveals that Piquant chickens were first brought to Louisiana in 1780 by a migrant chicken plucker named Piquant. Unable to find employment, he soon began plucking his own chickens, and (being careless in the way he walked) stumbled across a delicious recipe, later to become known as 'Chicken Piquant'!

1 Young Hen	1 Bell Pepper, Chopped
1 Can Petit Pois	½ Cup Celery, Chopped
1 Can Buttered Mushrooms	2 Pods Garlic, Minced
	2 Pods Pimento, Mashed
1 Small Can Tomato Paste	⅛ Tsp. Ground Cloves
	¼ Tsp. Oregano
3 Tblsp. Butter	2 Tblsp. Parsley, Minced
2 Tblsp. Oil	Salt, Blk. Pepper &
2 Tblsp. Flour	Tabasco (to make hot
½ Cup Onions, Chopped	and peppery)
1 Tsp. Paprika	Boiling Water

Cut chicken into serving pieces. Fry in hot butter in heavy iron skillet over medium fire. Brown quickly, remove from skillet and keep warm. Add oil to drippings—when hot, add flour and brown. Add paprika, onion, celery, garlic, bell pepper and cook until tender. Add tomato sauce, pimentos, cloves, oregano, black pepper and Tabasco sauce, then add mushrooms. Finally add chicken and boiling water—just enough to cover chicken. Cover and simmer until chicken is tender. Drain petit pois and add to chicken, then add parsley the last 3 to 4 minutes. Serves six generously.

CHICKEN SALAD DELUXE

Chicken salad was discovered one day when a terrified young hen was trying desperately to escape from an over-sexed rooster that was pursuing her. She was holding her own until she tripped over a portable phonograph the other chickens were listening to, and fell headlong into a vat of boiling water, which literally stripped the meat from her bones. The farmer happened to witness her demise, and being a very frugal man, proceeded to coin a phrase, "Waste not—want not". He removed the feathers, threw in some seasoning and said, "Might as well make some chicken salad—deluxe, I guess".

1 Young Hen, or Large Springer	1½ Cups Mayonnaise
3 Cups Celery, Chopped	½ Tsp. Paprika
½ Lb. Lean Pork	1 Tblsp. Parsley, Minced
4 Hard Boiled Eggs	1 Tblsp. Vinegar
3 Tblsp. Green Onion Tops, Chopped	1 Small Dill Pickle, Diced
2-3 Doz. Stuffed Olives, Sliced	½ Lemon (juice of) Salt & Pepper to Taste

Cut chicken and pork in pieces and boil in 2 tblsp. chopped onions and 1 tsp. poultry seasoning until very tender. Cool and strip meat from bones, cut into bite size, salt and pepper, and sprinkle with lemon juice. Add chopped ingredients, sprinkle paprika and mix. Add mayonnaise, pickle, vinegar and eggs and toss lightly. If more tartness is preferred, add more vinegar.

P.S. Broth from chicken may be used for soups or gravies.

 # CREOLE POULTRY STUFFING

Some Creoles used to stuff their poultry by holding them around the neck and cramming food down their throat with the thumb. This was known as 'poultry stuffing'. It made them weigh more and they brought more money on the poultry market. This practice has long since been outlawed, but unbeknownst to their owners, some gluttonous poultry still continue to stuff themselves until they can hardly walk!

Giblets from 3 or 4 Chickens	10 Slices Stale French Bread
2 Onions, Chopped Fine	3 Hard Boiled Eggs, Diced
1 Sml. Gr. Pepper, Chopped	2 Tblsp. Parsley, Minced
2 Pods Garlic, Minced	1 Tsp. Paprika
2-3 Tsp. Butter	1 Tblsp. Worcestershire
½ Tsp. Poultry Seasoning	Salt
	Tabasco to Taste

Boil giblets in 3 cups of water seasoned with 1 celery stalk, 1 small onion, 1 pod of garlic and ½ tsp. poultry seasoning. Cover and boil gently until gizzards are tender, adding more water if needed. Strain broth and save for stuffing.

Chop giblets—soak bread in broth and squeeze very dry. Set aside. Heat 2 tblsp. butter in heavy skillet (low heat) and fry onions, garlic, green peppers and paprika until soft—add additional butter and fry squeezed bread **until golden brown,** chopping it and mixing constantly. Add giblets, mixing well—if too stiff, add a little broth—stir. Add Worcestershire sauce, salt, pepper and chopped eggs—mix. Add the parsley last.

HINT: I wash and freeze giblets. When I get 3 or 4 sets, I make this delicious stuffing as a side dish.

miscellaneous & desserts

BEEF BROTH BOUILLON ASPIC SALAD

Broth comes from the Irish 'bruith' (to boil), and is described as a liquid in which meat, barley, rice, vegetables, or the like have been gently boiled—a thin or simple soup. By simply adding 'er' to broth you have a brother. Brother is a person, usually not your sister, having the same parents as you do. If you add 'el' to broth, you have a brothel, which is a house of lewdness or ill fame, a house frequented by prostitutes (and people who frequent prostitutes); a bawdy house. This sounds like a lot more fun than having a brother or drinking thin soup!

1 Can Beef Bouillon
1 Pkg. Knox Gelatine
1 Can Artichoke Bottoms
1 Cup Gr. Beans, Cut Fine
1 Cup Pimento Stuffed Olives, Cut Fine
1 Tsp. Lee & Perrins
1 Tsp. Lemon Juice

Heat bouillon and water. Dissolve gelatine in ½ cup cold water and add to bouillon. Add Lee & Perrins and lemon juice. (This should measure 1 pt.). Place **one** artichoke bottom into 6 or 8 individual molds, then the green beans and olives mixed. Pour bouillon-gelatine over the vegetables and refrigerate. Serve on shredded lettuce with mayonnaise.

SAUSAGE-NOODLE CASSEROLE

Sausage is described as meat, usually pork, minced and highly seasoned, commonly forced into a tubular case (it won't go in there by itself, you know) made of the prepared intestines of some animal (think of these things when you eat sausage), which is tied shut at short intervals (I'd say about every 15 minutes) to form a string of plump cylindrical sections with rounded ends. The Noodle, on the other hand, is German for 'brain'. For example: "Use your noodle, you dumbkoff!"

1 Lb. Bulk Sausage	1 Can Tomato Sauce
½ Pkg. Noodles	1 Onion, Sliced Thin
1 Can Tomatoes	1 Cup Grated Cheese

Mix tomatoes and tomato sauce together. Fry sausage in little flat patties, drain all fat and set aside. Cook noodles until tender and drain. Place layer of noodles in casserole, then 4 or 5 sausage patties, ½ of cheese, ½ of onions and ½ tomato mixture. Repeat in same order. Bake for 30 minutes or until top is golden. May be prepared ahead and refrigerated.

SOPA DE ALBONDIGAS

Sopa De Albondigas, may his tribe increase
Awoke one night and thought of his niece
Who did all the cooking that brought him much
   peace
But not only that—it made him obese!
He said, "I'll get thinner to see how I look",
He even went out and bought him a book
On diets and calories—but he made one mistook,
He said, "Darn that woman, she's too good a cook!"

¾ Lb. Ground Chuck Beef	3 Tblsp. Butter
½ Lb. Ground Pork (lean)	2 Tsp. Paprika
1 Egg, Beaten	4-5 Drops Tabasco Sauce
¼ Cup Raw Rice	½ Tsp. Oregano
½ Tsp. Chili Powder	2 Tblsp. Mint Flakes
1 Cup Tomato Sauce	Salt & Pepper to Taste
1 Large Onion, Minced	5 Pts. Beef Stock or
3 Pods Garlic, Minced	(6 Boullion Cubes)

If bouillon cubes are used, dissolve in 5 pts. (10 full cups) of boiling water and set aside. Mix pork and beef thoroughly, then mix rice, egg, salt & pepper and mold into tiny balls. Heat butter in skillet, saute onions and garlic until soft (not brown). Lightly brown the meatballs—add tomato sauce, oregano, paprika, chili powder, Tabasco sauce, salt & pepper (lightly until tasted) and cook 5 minutes. Toss all into soup pot containing boiling bouillon. Cover and simmer 30 minutes. Add mint flakes just before serving and cook 5 minutes more. Serves 6.

"QUICKIE" SKILLET CASSEROLE

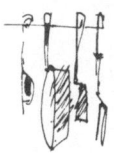

The "Quickie" was invented in 1785 by the Marquis de Quick right after having a sordid affair with an ostrich. Famished for food, he begged his cook for some nourishment immediately. Not knowing exactly what the Marquis had in mind (him being so weird and all) she frantically threw everything she had on the stove into one large pot. It turned out simply delicious, and, having been revived, the Marquis went on to have numerous other affairs. This is the original recipe that brought him the strength he so desperately needed!

1 7 Oz. Pkg. Macaroni with Cheese	2 Pods Garlic, Minced
1 Lb. Ground Beef	1 Cup Canned Tomatoes
2 Tblsp. Coooking Oil	½ Cup Tomato Sauce
1 Large Onion, Chopped	1 Tblsp. Parsley, Minced
½ Bell Pepper, Chopped	¼ Tsp. Oregano
	Salt to Taste

Brown meat quickly in hot oil; remove meat from skillet, keeping it warm. Fry the chopped vegetables in the drippings from the meat until soft and pulpy (not brown). Add tomatoes, cook for 5 minutes, then add tomato sauce and oregano. Add meat, blending well and let cook 5 minutes more, then add parsley. Prepare macaroni as per directions on package. When drained, add to meat mixture—if too thick, add a little hot water. Sprinkle top with ½ the contents of the cheese package.

CASSEROLE SUPREME
(Made With Left-Overs)

When the Thanksgiving dinner is over,
And your cooking is done for the day,
Seldom is heard a discouraging word,
For what can antelope say?

3 Cups Turkey (or
    Chicken) in bite-sized
    pieces
2-3 Cups Dressing,
    Crumbled
½ Cup Left-Over Gravy
3½ Cups Milk

½ Cup Pecans or
    Almonds, Chopped
4-5 Drops Tabasco
½ Tsp. Paprika
1 Small Pkg. Egg Noodles
½ Cup Bread Crumbs,
    Seasoned

Cook egg noodles, drain. Put dressing in bottom of casserole. Spread chicken or turkey over top, pour on gravy and sprinkle with pecans (or almonds). Spread noodles next and add milk. Cover with bread crumbs. Lightly dash with Tabasco sauce and paprika. Bake at 325° until thoroughly heated, approximately 30 minutes. Serves 8 to 10. Sliced black olives and finely chopped pimento may be added for color.

This delicious casserole is peachy to serve the Sunday after Thanksgiving (or the 4th of July)—unless you had ham, of course.

A SAUCY CREOLE DRESSING

If the day is a bit depressing,
And you have nothing that is pressing,
Why don't you try this Creole dressing?

And here's a fact that we keep stressing,
Some call this recipe a blessing,
Cause you can leave out all the guessing.

Up pops a thought you've been surpressing,
How many of you are confessing,
You prefer a **saucy Creole undressing?**

1 Lb. Pork Sausage	1 Large Onion, Chopped
½ Lb. Ground Beef	1½ Cup Celery, Chopped
3 Tblsp. Butter or Bacon Drippings	2 Tblsp. Parsley, Minced
2 Tblsp. Oil	½ Tsp. Sage
10 Slices Stale French Bread (soak in milk and squeeze dry)	½ Tsp. Kitchen Seasoning
4 Hard Boiled Eggs	3 Pods Garlic, Minced
	1 Tblsp. Paprika
	Salt & Pepper to Taste

Fry meat in hot bacon drippings (or oil) in heavy pot until brown, not dry. Add paprika, onions, celery, garlic—cook and stir over low heat for 15 minutes. Add butter to mixture and then the soaked bread—fry until brown and well blended. Add sage and kitchen seasoning, parsley, salt and pepper to taste—add a few dashes of cayenne, if desired. Mix—add a little hot water if too stiff. Finally, add diced eggs and mix gently. This makes a delicious dressing to use with poultry or as a side dish.

EGGPLANT—SPANISH STYLE

Here we have the Eggplant again, this time prepared for people who like things a little spicier, especially their eggplant. This recipe is not recommended for people with ulcers, chronic kidney disturbances, or those prone to Mexican heartburn!

2 Eggplant, med. sized
½ Lb. Ground Pork
6 Hot Chorice (Mexican Hot Sausage) cut in pieces
1 Cup Onions, Chopped
3 Pods Garlic, Chopped
3 Tblsp. Butter
¼ Cup Tomato Paste
2 Pimentos, Chopped
1 Bell Pepper, cut in rings
1 Tsp. Paprika
6 Drops Tabasco Sauce
2-3 Dashes Chili Powder
¼ Cup Water
Salt & Pepper to Taste

Peel and dice eggplant—set aside. Heat butter in large pot over medium heat; fry pork, garlic, onions and paprika, using low heat. Add hot chorice, tomato paste, pimentos and bell pepper. Add diced eggplant, 2 or 3 dashes of chili powder, salt, pepper and Tabasco sauce to taste. Add ¼ cup of hot water. Cover tightly and cook until eggplant is tender, stirring often. Serve with steamed rice.

STEWED EGGPLANT—PLANTATION STYLE

According to Webster, the Eggplant is a widely cultivated East Indian herb (Solanum Melongena) allied to the potato (that means they fought together), blue-red in color, which is cooked and served as a vegetable. (During World War II, the government subsidized an Egg Plant near Edgard, La., but it never got off the ground.) The Eggplant is considered a delicacy and is widely consumed in the South, along with anything else that walks, grows, swims or crawls.

1 1-lb. Slice Ham, Diced	3 Tblsp. Oil
2 Eggplants, Med. Sized	½ Tsp. Paprika
8 Green Onions, Chopped	1 Tblsp. Lee & Perrins
1 Pod Garlic, Minced	1 Tblsp. Lemon Juice
1 Sml. Can Tomatoes, Chopped	3 Tblsp. Parsley, Minced
2 Sprigs Thyme	¼ Cup Hot Water
	Salt & Pepper to Taste

Peel eggplant, dice and set aside. Heat oil in large pot, fry green onions, paprika, garlic (low heat) until soft —add tomatoes, thyme, ham, stirring constantly. Add eggplant, lemon juice and water. Salt and pepper to taste, add Lee and Perrins. Cook until eggplant is tender and then add parsley. Serve over hot steamed rice.

GUACAMOLE AVOCADO SALAD

The avocado is a pulpy, green or purple edible fruit of certain tropical American trees of the Laurel family (the Hardy family has some nice trees, too). In the South, the avocado is known as the alligator pear—which may be the reason you seldom see an alligator alone—they always travel in 'pears'!

2 Avocados, Very Ripe	1 Tblsp. White Onion,
2 Tblsp. Lemon Juice	Minced
2 Tsp. Olive Oil	2 Tblsp. Green Chile
1 Ripe Tomato, Large	Peppers, Peeled
1 Pod Garlic, Crushed	½ Tsp. Salt & Black Pepper
Shredded Lettuce	(to taste)

Rub bowl with garlic pod and discard (not the bowl). Peel and remove seed from avocados and mash; cover immediately with lemon juice to prevent discoloring. Add tomato and other ingredients. Mix, serve on shredded lettuce with crisp tortillas or oyster crackers.

FRENCH STYLE GREEN BEANS
(Au Croutons)

This recipe first came to light,
While cooking his green beans one night,
A Frenchman with too much to drink,
Was making croutons by the sink,
He slipped and fell—then the latter
Ended up on his green bean platter!

2 Pkgs. Frozen Beans	6 Slices Very Stale Bread
1 Slice Ham, Diced	(diced and fried brown)
8 Green Onion Tops	1 Tblsp. Parsley
1 Tblsp. Tomato Paste	Salt & Pepper
2 Tblsp. Butter	

Cook green beans as per directions on package and set aside. Heat butter in pot—fry green onions slightly—add tomato sauce and diced ham. Let cook about 5 minutes on low heat. Add mixture to beans—add salt & pepper—stir and cook 2 or 3 minutes. Add parsley. Butter slices of bread and dice, then brown the cubes in heavy skillet using low heat—add more butter or margarine if necessary. Serve beans on wide platter and spread croutons on top of beans just before serving. Delicious with boiled new potatoes (parslied).

SPICY GINGERBREAD—SOUTHERN STYLE

2 Eggs	½ Tsp. Baking Powder
¾ Cup Brown Molasses	2 Tsp. Ginger
¾ Cup Brown Sugar	1 Tsp. Cinnamon
¾ Cup Shortening	½ Tsp. Powdered Cloves
2½ Cups Flour	½ Tsp. Grated Nutmeg
2 Tsp. Soda	1 Cup Boiling Water

Cream shortening and sugar, add beaten eggs and molasses. Then add all dry ingredients which have been sifted together with flour. Add boiling water last. Can be baked in loaf pan or muffin tins in moderate oven about 30 minutes, or, when an inserted toothpick comes out clean. If it comes out dirty, throw the whole mess away and start over; or just keep sticking toothpicks into it until they come out clean!

FRENCH PECAN NOUGAT

1½ Cups White Granulated Sugar	1 Cup Pecans—Must Be Finely Chopped

Melt sugar in **heavy** skillet, keep stirring. When golden brown syrup is formed, add pecans. Stir, then pour onto well-buttered surface—a large flat dish, a marble top table, a cookie sheet, or your husband's head. Be sure to melt sugar slowly over low heat. (This recipe was given to me by my Grandmother, who had a heck of a time trying to get rid of it!)

ENID'S CREAMY PECAN PRALINES

1½ Cups Brown Sugar, Light or Golden Preferably	1½ Cups Pecan Meats, Halves or Broken Pieces
1 Cup White Granulated Sugar	½ Cup Evaporated Milk
	1 Tsp. Vanilla Extract
	¼ Tsp. Salt

Combine all ingredients in a heavy pot—then jump in with them! Cook slowly, stirring constantly until mixture reaches soft-ball stage (then choose up sides and have a little game). Test syrup in cold water as mixture thickens. Remove from heat. Let cool slightly, beat a few times (until it's sorry), then drop tablespoon-sized quantities onto buttered sheets of waxed paper, spreading and shaping into cookie-type rounds. When sufficiently cooled and hardened, lift from waxed paper gently. Throw away and eat the waxed paper!

CHERRY CHEESE PIE

Since this pie contains Graham crackers, we will give you a short history on the Graham cracker. Graham is an entire-wheat flour which was stumbled across over a century ago by Alexander Bell Graham, a used windmill salesman, who had a bad case of leprosy. While strolling through a wheat field one day, his nose fell off, and, while stooping down to retrieve his nose (to keep as a souvenir, more or less), he noticed that the wheat he had trampled had ground into a brownish powder. Amazed, he rushed some to the local miller, who was in the grain room teaching his new secretary how to grind, and found that he had discovered a new flour. Since they were already using it to make Graham crackers, they gave it his name, 'Graham'!

| 1½ Cups Graham Cracker Crumbs | ½ Cup Margarine |
| | 2 Tsp. Sugar |

Blend crumbs, margarine and sugar and press into pie plate or tin, and bake 10 minutes at 350° in oven.

FILLING

1 Large Philadelphia Cream Cheese	½ Cup Lemon Juice
⅔ Can Sweetened Condensed Milk	1 Tsp. Vanilla with dash Nutmeg
1 Tblsp. Sugar	1 Large. can Cherry Pie Filling

Whip all ingredients, except cherries, into a thick consistency. Pour into crust. Pour cherry pie filling on top and chill in refrigerator for several hours before serving. This one is a fuse-blower!

CHERRIES JUBILEE

The Cherry is described as any of several species of Prunus, having globose drupes enclosing a smooth stone. This is believed to have originated the old saying "A smooth stone gathers no globose drupes". In Europe, the Cherry was worshipped and glorified (and even held in high esteem) from 1780 until 1820, known as the 'Cherry Years'. The Cherry was considered to be very lucky and dried Cherry pits were strung like beads and worn about the neck to ward off the plague, cholera and bad breath. On the 50th birthday of the Cherry, some villagers got together and said, "Let's throw a Jubilee"! This is reputed to have been the origin of Cherries Jubilee.

1 Cup Pitted Sweet Bing Cherries	2 Tblsp. Kirsch Liqueur Vanilla Ice Cream
¼ Cup Brandy	

Add the ¼ cup of warm brandy to the pitted cherries. Set brandy afire and when flame dies down, add the liqueur. Heat and serve on vanilla ice cream.

For a simple Cherries Jubilee: add cherry liquid to 2 tsp. of sugar and 2 tsp. cornstarch. Heat slowly—stir until it thickens. Add cherries and one tblsp. brandy and a couple dashes of nutmeg or mace. Serve warm over crepes or vanilla ice cream.

PEACH OR APPLE COBBLER

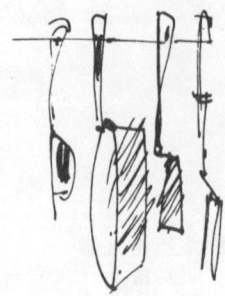

A cobbler fixes many shoes
That much we can't deny.
But how can anyone fix shoes,
While baked inside a pie?

2 Large Cans Sliced Peaches (or apples)	⅔ Cup Shortening
2 Cups Flour	5-6 Tblsp. Ice Cold Milk
1 Tsp. Salt	6 Tblsp. Butter

Sift flour and salt together **twice** in mixing bowl, add shortening and blend together with two forks or the hands (two). Add cold milk and blend. Divide in half. Roll one half and place in casserole. Bake and let cool. Drain peaches (or apples) and place one layer in casserole and add 2 tblsp. sugar. Roll out other half of dough and cut into 1 or 2 inch strips. Place layer of strips over peaches, add more peaches and 2 tblsp. more of sugar, then repeat process, making at least 3 layers. On last layer, also place dough around edge of casserole. Bake at 350° for 45 minutes, or until crust is golden.

For sauce, add 2 tblsp. sugar and 1 tblsp. cornstarch to peach juice. Cook several minutes until it begins to thicken slightly, then add a little butter. Serve sauce **hot.**

NONPAREIL CUSTARD BREAD PUDDING

Nonpareil means 'having no equal' which, of course, pertains to this pudding. A custard is 'a sweetened mixture of milk and eggs', which may be prepared in various flavors. But how many of you remember Custard's Last Stand, or his famous last words as he lay dying near his great stallion, "Horsie", after suffering bitter defeat at the hands of Sitting Bull? Our research department obtained this statement from a direct descendant of Old Funky Legs, an Indian warrior who took part in the battle. General Custard's last words were, "Man, I sure could use a sweetened mixture of milk and eggs right now"!

2 Cups Milk, Scalded	½ Cup Raisins (soaked in milk)
1 Cup Evaporated Milk	
⅓ Cup Cond. Milk, Sweetened	2½ Cups Stale French Bread, cubed
¼ Cup Sugar	¼ Tsp. Cinnamon
3 Large Eggs	¼ Tsp. Allspice
3 Tblsp. Butter	½ Tsp. Nutmeg
	2 Tsp. Vanilla Ext.

Cut stale bread into small cubes, set aside. Scald milk, don't boil. Cream butter with fork in suitable bowl, add evaporated milk, then hot milk and butter. Stir in spices one at a time, add vanilla and mix well. Pour pudding mixture into well-buttered baking dish. Stir in cubed bread and let soak at least 15 minutes. Gently push raisins down into mixture leaving a few on top. Place pudding dish in pan of **hot** water and bake in oven at 350° about 1 hour, or until firm.

TOPPING: HARD SAUCE WITH WHISKEY

⅔ Cup Butter	⅔ Cup Sugar
1 Jigger Whiskey	

Place butter in small deep bowl (slightly warm) and cream with fork until light in color. Add sugar, 1 scant tblsp. at a time, stirring constantly and cream mixture for few minutes more. DO NOT REFRIGERATE. Just before serving, blend in 1 jigger (or more, to taste) of whiskey and whip in thoroughly until fluffy. Top servings of pudding with 1 tblsp. Hard Sauce.

PECAN PIE

The Pecan is the smooth, oblong, thin-shelled nut of the hickory species (named after General Andrew Jackson), which grows in the south-central United States. The Pecan tree possesses hard, brittle wood (hence, pecan brittle) and attains giant size in Texas, along with everything else. The Pecan is widely used in Southern cooking, mainly in desserts and candies. The Pecan is very nourishing and small groups of migratory monkeys have subsisted on nothing but the pecan until rescued by lesser-known animals.

⅔ Cup Light Brown Sugar, packed	1 Tsp. Vanilla
1¼ Cups Pecans	1 Cup Dark Corn Syrup
3 Whole Eggs	½ Cup Light Corn Syrup
2 Tblsp. Butter, Melted	⅛ Tsp. Salt
2 Tblsp. (level) Flour	1 Unbaked Pastry Pie Shell

Beat eggs, blend in melted butter, flour, vanilla, salt, sugar and syrup. Sprinkle nuts over bottom of unbaked pastry shell. Gently pour syrup mixture over nuts. Bake at 425° for 10 minutes, then at 350° for about 40 minutes.

TID-BIT BALLS

2-3 Small Pkg. Rice Krispies	2 Tblsp. Brown Sugar
	¼ Cup White Sugar
2 Cups (scant) Molasses	2 Tblsp. Butter
	1 Tsp. Cinnamon

Cook sugar and molasses together until a hard ball is formed by dropping in cold water. Stir in butter and cinnamon & set aside. Empty Rice Krispies into bowl and pour mix over them, stirring and mixing until well coated. Let cool. Grease fingers and roll into small balls (if you can roll your fingers into small balls, you're pretty good), then lay on waxed paper for 4 hours. While you're laying on the waxed paper you might take a little nap!

NUTTY RUM BALLS

3 Cups Ground Vanilla Wafers	½ Cup Rum
1½ Cups Ground Pecans	1 Cup Confectioners Powdered Sugar

Mix wafers, pecans and Rum into a paste, then stand in refrigerator for an hour (or until you're cold). Pinch off small pieces and roll into little balls. Roll a day before eating. Or you can drink the Rum and forget the whole thing!

PAIN PERDU
(LOST BREAD)

Our research man informs us that Pain Perdu is not an anatomical discomfort—such as Pain in the Perdu—as we first believed, but that it really means 'Lost Bread'. This phrase may have originated in any number of logical ways, leaving us unsure as to which is authentic. However, we do have reason to believe that originally the French referred to money lost in a crap game (or poker game, or being rolled) as 'Lost Bread'. Other sources say this should actually be 'Lost French Bread', but that's another story.

6 Slices Stale French Bread	½ Tsp. Vanilla Extract
2 Small Eggs, Well Beaten	Few Dashes of Cinnamon
1 Cup Evaporated Milk	& Nutmeg
2 Tsp. Brown Sugar	2 Tblsp. Powdered Sugar

Combine beaten eggs, milk, sugar, spices and vanilla in a suitable sized bowl or pan and beat thoroughly. Soak each slice of stale bread in the mixture and brown in a heavy skillet, using a little butter or margarine. Sprinkle with powdered sugar and serve while hot. A delicious breakfast treat for those you love (or even for those you don't love)!

"QUICKIE" VANILLA ICE CREAM
(or, who's for a "Quickie"?)

1 Qt. Milk	1 Egg Yolk, Well Beaten
1 Pt. Whipped Cream	3 Tblsp. Sugar (or to taste)
½ Can Sweetened	1 Tblsp. Vanilla
Cond. Milk	Few Dashes Nutmeg
1 Can Evaporated Milk	

Using large bowl—to well-beaten egg yolk (if you don't have any well-beaten eggs, just find a well-beaten chicken and hang around until she lays one), add condensed milk and evaporated milk (one gets thicker while the other disappears). Thin with quart of milk, then add whipped cream. Mix thoroughly, add nutmeg & vanilla, mix again, then freeze. Serves 8 generously. You may vary the recipe by adding almond flavoring and crushed peaches in place of vanilla.

This was a favorite recipe of my roly poly Aunt Josie, who never quite attained the height of 5 feet; in fact, she was only 3 foot, 6 inches on her tallest day. She was famous throughout the countryside for her delicious "shortie" desserts—because of her size, I guess.

mother's little kitchen kuties for bewildered brides

1. Never forget to take your pill!

2. Remember the "3—S's": Sear, Saute and Scald.
   Sear: To brown quickly in **hot** oil or fat.
   Saute: To fry lightly and quickly, using little fat,
   turning frequently.
   Scald: Just under the boiling point.

3. Vegetables must be refrigerated immediately
   after purchasing (like on the way home) to stay
   fresh.

4. Never buy wilted or 'tired-looking' vegetables.
   They've had it! Vegetables must be crisp and
   fresh looking, and please don't overcook them—
   steam them over low heat in a tightly covered
   pot. Add just a tablespoonful of water to start
   them steaming.

5. Rub your salad bowl with a piece of crushed
   garlic to give a tantalizing flavor to greens or
   potato salad.

6. Never wash a wooden salad bowl—wipe it out
   with a clean cloth or a piece of soft bread (then
   wash the bread)!

7. Use different shades of greens to give an interesting look to salads. People will say, "My, that's
   an interesting looking salad."

8. A slow oven is 300°—a moderate oven (never
   use a liberal oven) is 350°—a hot oven is 400 to
   500°. Anything over that is an exploded oven.

9. Cook an average 4 to 5 lb. beef roast at 300° (medium rare) allowing 20 to 25 minutes per lb. You will have less shrinkage and a more juicy and tender roast.
   Pork must be cooked 40 to 45 minutes per lb.
   Veal must be cooked 35 to 40 minutes per lb.
   Stuffed chicken, roasted, 35 min. per lb. at 325°.
   Cold Cuts: 0 minutes per lb.

10. To cut down on baking time of potatoes, boil 15 minutes and grease before placing in oven. Heating clear through makes the difference.

11. Before broiling or frying a chicken, rub it inside and out with a wedge of lemon. (Give it a thrill —it will never have another one.)

12. For a little "fuzz" on a chicken, singe with a lighted candle. I used to use an electric razor, but it was hard to get around the nose!

13. When preparing a chicken, remove surplus fat and render it (helpless) immediately over low heat. Pour into container and refrigerate. It adds much flavor and richness to Creole cuisine.

14. Save bacon drippings for seasoning vegetables, etc. Keep in refrigerator.

15. Add a teaspoon of vegetable oil and a teaspoon of lemon juice to water when cooking rice.

16. When cheese becomes too dried out, grate it for future use in casseroles, spaghetti and fruit salads. Store in tightly covered jar, refrigerate.

17. Never buy a smooth, shiny egg (steal them)—a fresh egg has a dull, slightly rough finish, which makes it kind of hard on the hen.

18. Crack and peel hard-boiled eggs under running water. (While you're taking a shower is fine.)

19. To determine the freshness of a fish, press with your fingers. If flesh remains depressed, you may be sure it didn't spend last night in the water!

20. To stretch a meat loaf, sprinkle crumbled 'quick oats' to mixed ingredients ($\frac{1}{2}$ cup to 1 lb. meat). It makes a delicious loaf. ('Don't let your meat loaf'—that just fractures me!)

21. For biscuits with a well-browned top, 'paint' them with a little whole milk. Skimmed milk won't do, neither will half milk.

22. A pre-baking hint: Grease your baking pan with a **little** vegetable oil and sprinkle with a bit of flour. A sure way to avoid sticking. Another sure way is not to bake at all!

23. A pie shell should be baked at 425° 12-15 minutes.

24. Make your guy a jiffy pie. Use the new milk chocolate pudding and follow directions on package, no matter what they say! Cool and pour into a baked pie shell. For serving, just top with whipped cream or jiffy whip. For a festive touch, squirt a little on his head!

25. Always place filled custard cups or puddings in shallow baking pan containing a small amount of **hot water.** This applies to my own "Nonpareil". Now you may go back to 'As The World Turns'.